BABY GIRL

BROWN

Cassandra Santiago

Dedication

First, I would like to thank God above for allowing me to live and share my story. I realize without Him I am nothing.

I would also like to thank my parents Clarence and Shirley Mack for choosing me. Without them, I would not be the person I am today. Rest in peace daddy.

To my children: Jeremai, Jerel, Joshua and Cierra, you are the reasons I didn't give up even when I wanted to.

My precious grandchildren: Jayce, little Jeremai, Jayla, Tyson, Jaylyn and Nyla. God gave me precious jewels when you were all born. I love you all more than words can say.

To my sister Yolanda, my nephew Trey, and my niece Breyona; no matter where this journey takes me, you will never be replaced. You all will always hold a special place in my heart.

To my best friend since second grade, Shelly. We are so much alike yet so different, but the one thing we have in common has finally come to light for the both of us. I wish you well and hope your outcome turns out to be as good as mine. We both have traveled this road so long, with so many obstacles in the way. We can finally see some light at the end of the tunnel. Thank you for always being there for me. You have been the best friend ever.

My special friend, Anthony D. Thanks for the encouraging words! It was you that said, "If you had not of been adopted, everyone that's in your life today, would have never been". That is a statement that always stuck with me.

Lastly, I would like to acknowledge my family from Philadelphia; my aunt, uncle, and all my cousins, the McKeither family who always showed me love no matter what. You all loved me when I didn't know how to love myself. You were there through thick and thin. You all were my protectors, my heroes, and some of my biggest supporters. I love you all.
Rest in peace, Debbie.

Introduction

Even to this day, I still have so many questions about myself, my identity. Questions to which I hope to find the answers. Why did it take 45 years for me to get to this point? Was this my destiny? Is there a purpose to all this? I know God doesn't give more than you can bear, but why did I have to bear this? Why should I bear the unknown? But I also know that, according to Psalms 37:4 (KJV) "Delight thyself also in the Lord; and he shall give thee the desires of thine heart." I have desired knowledge of myself for 44 years, and it is finally coming to pass. But there are still so many questions that haunt me. Why did my great aunt offer to adopt me but later change her mind? Still so many questions and I have yet to find answers. But I have faith that God knows the plans He has for me, for good and not disaster. Maybe in due time all will be revealed. This is my story.

Chapter 1
The Burst Bubble

Growing up, for the first five years of my life, I was the only child. I was daddy's little girl and I was in my own little world. My parents named me Cassandra. I liked my name but, when I started talking, I couldn't pronounce my name. Since I couldn't say it well, the nickname 'Sand' came about. According to my mother, everyone seemed to adore me as a baby. My mother and father's closest friends would bring me gifts and visit for hours at a time. I was told I wanted for nothing. I had everything I needed and more. I was blessed beyond measure.

The year I turned five was one of the most memorable years of my life. I remember there were three foster children brought to our home late one evening. Two girls and a baby boy. I didn't quite understand why, but my mother explained that they were children who were less fortunate than us and they needed somewhere to stay for a while. I found myself feeling a little jealous because

I was the only child for five years, and I wanted it to stay that way. I was worried about how things would change, but I never imagined how drastically it would impact my life.

Shortly after that, I remember another baby being brought to our home. A beautiful baby girl; that baby was Londie, my "forever younger sister," who is five years younger than me. From what I can remember, things remained okay on the home front, even after the new arrivals. It wasn't until my foster sisters and I started school when my perfect world ended up turning upside down.

One day in school, when I was in the first grade, a kid came up to me and asked why I was so dark-skinned, and my foster sisters were so light-skinned. Being young and naïve, I didn't really have an answer except that they were foster children. They weren't blood relatives. Well, I guess my answer was not enough. That same kid went back to my foster sisters and asked them that same question. Apparently, they had the right answer. A seemingly better answer. They quickly replied, "She was adopted." As I think back, that was one of the worst days of my life. At least that's what I thought at the time. That same kid came back, again, this time with many other kids teasing me about being adopted. My little six-year-old self was crushed! I remember crying and just wanting to rush home to my parents. This could not be true. Everyone used to say I looked just like my father. Apparently, that was not true either. How could I look like someone with whom I didn't share any DNA? No, those kids must be lying! And, I could not wait to get home to tell my mother the ugly lie my foster sisters had told. Everything was fine, until they came along.

Instantly I started to hate them. It was all their fault that this assumed lie had come out. I remember running into the house, crying, and I said, "Mom my sisters told the kids at school I was adopted, and everyone started teasing me!" My mother's response was simple and unnerving. She replied calmly, "You were. Why are you crying?" I thought to myself, 'are you serious? Why am I crying?' Why was I crying? That moment right there changed my life forever. I wasn't the same after that. I was sad, hurt, confused, angry, and embarrassed all at the same time. My world had just been turned upside down. My perfect little bubble had burst and there was no going back.

So many questions ran through my head. So many emotions running wild in my heart. How can this be? How can my perfect world turn in a flash? How could I go from looking just like my dad, to being adopted? Nothing made sense. I cried endlessly. My mother tried comforted me the best way she could, but nothing my mother said after the words "you were" mattered to me. I just couldn't get past those two words, so little yet so life-changing.

Chapter 2
Mad at the World

My mom tried to explain this whole thing out. But even her explanation had upset me further, in that moment. She said, "Sand, we had decided we were never going to tell you that you were adopted." What? I was completely devastated. What weighed heavily on me the most was the fact that the foster kids knew but I didn't. How can these strangers know more about me than me?

It wasn't until later that I found out, DYFUS usually gives the foster children a little background information on the family they would be staying with before they come into a home. I recall asking my mother so many questions. Why did the foster kids have to come here? Why wasn't she going to ever tell me I was adopted? Why was I adopted in the first place? Why didn't I stay with my real family? (I was too young to understand they were my real family.) Why didn't they want me? My mother said to me very calmly, "You should be happy you were adopted. You were chosen. When your father and I went to look at the babies you were the only one smiling, so we chose you."

But I wasn't happy, nothing she said could comfort me or justify what had just happened. Nothing could make me feel better. I was deeply scarred. Thinking about that moment in my life brings tears to my eyes now. I later learned my father couldn't have children, so my parents made the decision to adopt. Later down the road, when I became a teenager, I asked my dad why he couldn't have children. He told me that his sperm count was just too low. The irony of it all. Out of seventeen children, my father was the only one that couldn't have children. I called it coincidence, but I know now, it was God orchestrating my life.

My father was a little different than my mother when I talked about being adopted. My mother did not show us many emotions, so I couldn't tell if it bothered her or not that I inquired about my biological family. My father seemed hurt that I wanted to know about the bloodline I originally came from. Although he didn't have any answers for me, I would see the sadness that overcame him when I would bring the subject up. Eventually, I stopped asking him questions because, as I got older, I realized it bothered him when I referenced my biological family.

Eventually, I became rebellious and resentful. I was mad at the world. It was as if having to restrain myself from discovering my real identity did something to me! I did not want to return to school. I was so ashamed. I was angry all the time. Every time my mother would piss me off, I would say, "You know what? I wish I hadn't been smiling the day you went to pick out a baby!" I was hurt, and hurt people hurt other people.

As the years went by, I became angrier and angrier. I would run away often and made it my mission to make my mother's life as miserable as possible. As I went into my teenage years, I believe things only got worse. I wanted to know where my parents were, and why didn't anyone in the family take me in? Why did I have to be adopted? Not only was I mad at my parents who were raising me, I was mad at my biological parents for not raising me. For some reason I felt like I wanted my real parents. In my little head, my parents were not my real parents anymore, because I was adopted. They were just people who took me in, this was my perception. I was just like one of the foster kids, away from their family.

Chapter 3
Spirit of Rejection

I felt that way for a long time, like I just didn't belong. Especially when things didn't go my way. I felt like my home was a temporary situation. Maybe soon, I'd find my real parents? But the only information I had was that my mother was fourteen when she had me, her father was raising her, and there was no mention of my father at the time. I had nothing else to go on. Not a single clue that could help me find my birth parents.

My birthdays affected me the most. Every birthday I would wonder if my biological mother remembered it's my birthday. 'Does she think about me at all? Will she ever look for me? Is she still alive? Where was her mother?' Since I knew nothing of my biological father, I wondered if he even knew I existed? Where was he? So many questions but no possible answers, (so I thought). This was my secret torture, the torment of my daily life. Nobody seemed to understand. They were on the outside looking in. They had their biological family.

I didn't have mine. My mother's family all accepted me and never made me feel like I wasn't part of the family, but in my heart, I knew there was no bloodline for me.

My father's side of the family is a whole different story, however. Some I felt comfortable with and some I felt like a stranger around. That still holds true to this day. I remember my grandmother, my father's mother, always saying, "we love you Sand, even if you were adopted." I don't know her heart behind what she said. I don't understand why she had to remind me that I was adopted. Although I never told her, her words had a very negative effect on me. Why couldn't I get a simple 'I love you, Sand?' I don't know if she meant it in a negative way, or if it was just her way of comforting me. Either way, it didn't help. If anything, it only made my hurt deeper. I never really had a close relationship with my father's mother, anyway. So, eventually, it didn't matter to me what she said or thought about me.

Actions speaks louder than any words. Everyone looked like someone in the family except me. I wanted to belong, I wanted to look like my sister or perhaps a cousin, but I didn't. People often told me that I looked just like my dad. That was a lie because he really wasn't my dad. He only took on the role of a dad, in my head. I remember, one day, looking through all my mother's important papers, trying to find answers to so many unanswered questions. I couldn't find anything. I realized my mother really didn't have any information on me or my biological family. I was totally lost, and I felt abandoned. The spirit of rejection was strong and not having any answers didn't help.

I thought about my birth mother often. I wondered what she looked like. Is she tall like I am, is she dark skinned, does she wear her hair long or short, did she age well, did she have any more kids? And, most importantly, does she think about me as much as I think about her? I thought about her all the time, always imagining her to look like me; picturing her reaction when we'd finally meet.

Why couldn't anybody in her family take me in? I had heard that her father was raising her. I wonder why her father was raising her. Where was her mother? When it came to my birth father, for some reason, I did not think or question much about him. I did wonder what might have been the circumstances. Was I the product of a one-night stand? Did my mother even tell him I existed? If he knew, did he have any say? Did he want me? Why didn't his family take me in?

I had so many questions as a child, and well into my adult life; but no answers. There was such a void in my life, that even now it seems unbearable. Who am I? Why am I here? Why did God allow this to happen to me? It's hard to understand when you haven't traveled the road I've traveled. Knowing that I was adopted weighed heavily on my heart most of my life. The road was long, hard, and often dark. Many times, I felt so alone and unwanted. Don't get me wrong, my parents that raised me gave my sister and me the best of everything. We lacked nothing. But for me, at that time in my life, it just was not good enough. I wanted my biological parents. I wanted to belong. I wanted for us all to look alike. Most of all, I wanted to stop the hurt of feeling rejected.

Chapter 4
Drowning in Sorrows

As far as I was concerned, back then, I wanted to have what every other family had. Needless to say, I had it all along, but I was too dumb and immature to realize it. I did have what other families had, and probably so much more. When you're young, it's hard to process the things that we consider tragedies. Yes, in my mind, this was a tragedy that left me devastated for many years of my life. It left me feeling insecure, unloved, unwanted, and abandoned. It left me in pain.

Every negative thing that I encountered I found myself paralleling it with being given up for adoption. My marriage, failed relationships, friendships that ended for whatever reason; all of it always made me think back to being unwanted or abandoned. My inner thoughts were, 'if my real parents didn't want me, nobody else does either.' It was 'woe is me' for such a long period of time in my life, constantly drowning in my own sorrows. What a horrible feeling! Can you imagine living a life that every day you wish you were somewhere or someone else? Can you imagine not even knowing who you really are? Looking at the many faces on the street, wondering if they were somehow related to you? Oftentimes, someone would say, "Oh, you look just like someone I know." Can you imagine wondering if that person they know was related to you in some kind of way?

For years, I walked around ashamed and embarrassed because I was adopted. The word adoption was such an ugly word to me. For the longest time, I associated adoption with not being wanted. Being adopted and being an orphan meant the same thing to me. Clearly, that was so far from true. As I matured, I learned the difference. I don't think I ever got over being adopted, but I learned to adapt.

Growing up, my mother was the disciplinarian of the family, but she loved and protected my sister and me at all cost. Was she overbearing? Absolutely! Did she take things to the extreme? No doubt! But now that I am older, I realize she was only making me the woman that I am today. So many times, I would think she is the meanest mother in the world, and I couldn't wait to get grown and move out. Now that I am grown with kids of my own, I am not singing that song anymore. She tolerated my foolishness for a very long time. As I think back, even I must admit that the hell I caused my mother was uncalled for. I did so many hateful and spiteful things just because life had thrown me a curve ball that I was not ready for and certainly did not know how to deal with.

If I knew then what I know now I would have cherished every moment of being a child because this thing called life is no joke. My mother had done the best she could for my sister and me. Heck, she chose me - the only baby that was smiling at the time - to give me a life that my biological parents could not. For that alone, I am forever grateful. My father on the other hand was the easy- going parent. I never recall him raising his voice or his hands at my sister or me. He was kind and loving, and always had an encouraging word. I had 30 years with him until his time on earth was no more. I remember him teaching me how to ride a bike. I remember waiting patiently for him to come home from work. Every morning, while he would get ready for work, I would wake up and we'd watch the Jackson Five cartoon together. I remember our family trips to Florida. I can still recall our trips to the Atlantic City Boardwalk.

I have so many good memories, yet I also have unpleasant memories of when I was trying to adapt to the mere fact I was adopted. And, I wasn't over that when I got hit with another painful life moment. When my father and mother decided to separate, the impact was hard on me once again. Although that was their issue, I couldn't help but to feel abandoned yet again. Everyone seemed to easily walk away from me. Why? Unfortunately, this is how I processed everything then.

Chapter 5
Finding My Family

Can you imagine being teased because of being adopted? Can you imagine the feeling of being unwanted as a child? It might seem more common now, but adoption wasn't a common situation when I was growing up. Today, it's normal and even encouraged to put a baby up for adoption or adopt one. But with the questions I had earlier, those are the feelings with which I had to grow up. I think that was the very reason I was so ashamed. I always felt like I stood out because I was adopted.

There weren't too many people who understood how I felt, as I mentioned it wasn't common. Everyone thought just because my parents were taking good care of me, I was supposed to ignore the fact that I was adopted. Like I was supposed to just be okay with it and move on. For me, however, it was just not that easy. My sister, Londie, wasn't in the same place I was in. I couldn't talk to her about my feelings. She could care less that she was adopted, or so it seemed. She was always that happy go lucky child with not a care in the world. It didn't seem to faze her. If adoption was an issue with her, she certainly didn't act that way. And, she didn't act out the way I did. Londie was, also, five years younger than me, so she didn't make for very good conversation. Then, as we got older, she just never spoke on it.

After some years went by, my best friend and I reconnected. It seemed like, no matter the situation, she could always relate in some way. We used to talk hours at a time on the phone and, often, she would spend the night at my house. We would converse about adoption and talk about finding my biological family. At the time it just seemed like we were two teenagers living in our own little fantasy world. Pursuing my dream of finding my biological family seemed hopeless considering I had nothing to go on. I didn't even know the hospital that I was born in. The only thing I knew was my birthdate and the city where I was born. How could those two pieces of information be of any help? It seemed impossible.

Truth be told, my best friend and I never gave up, even when we became adults. We kept the faith and continued talking about the possibilities. After I grew up and got married, some of the hurt and shame went away. I was finally getting over the fact I was adopted. In my mind I was never going to find my biological family, and I needed to come to terms with it. I was starting to be okay with it but, every so often, my best friend and I would revisit the conversation about finding my family. Habakkuk 2:2 (KJV) says, "And the Lord answered me, and said, Write the vision, and make it plain upon tables, that he may run that readeth it." So, I always write down the things that I hope to accomplish. Finding my biological family was one of the things I had written down just last year. I didn't know how it was going to happen, but I kept the faith. I'll admit my faith was as small as a mustard seed but, then again, mustard seed faith was all I needed.

Chapter 6
A New Chapter

I often dreamed of meeting my biological parents at least one time. I think I wanted that more than anything else. One day I had a meeting with a DYFUS worker because I was anticipating doing foster care. One of the questions she asked me was, 'Why do you want to do foster care?' My response was because I was adopted and, although I am not ready to adopt, I do want to foster and give a child a decent home. I was fortunate enough to have parents who adopted me and gave me a nice home. The worker said, "Do you know where your parents are?" I replied, "No, but I would like to find them." She asked me if I knew where I was born? I said, "Yes. I do." She said, "Do you know the hospital?" Again, I could feel the bits of hope leaving my heart as I replied, "No."

But then, she said, "I can give you the application to get your original birth certificate, if you'd like." Suddenly, my face was flushed with an indescribable warmth and I was so excited, I didn't know how to react. I believe God answered my prayers when the Governor of New Jersey changed the law, where now any past adoption could be reopened, and the adoptee could request their original birth certificate in the State of New Jersey. This was no coincidence; it was nothing but God!

A few days later, the counselor stopped by the house to drop off the application and, anxiously, I filled it out. There was a phone number on the application, so I decided to call to verify the information the DYFUS worker had told me. There was no time for false hope, this time, I needed to be sure! The lady on the phone told me that they would send my original birth certificate, but that there was a big chance my parents' name would not be on it. I took a deep breath and said, "Miss, that's a chance I am willing to take."

That day, a new journey began for me. Although my children knew I was adopted, they had never known how I felt about being adopted. They never knew my struggles or the feelings that came with being adopted. The day I filled out my application was the same day I sent a group text to all four of my children. On August 22, 2018; I sent this text to my children, "Today starts a new chapter in my life! As you all know, I was adopted a little after birth. Majority of my life I have felt that I didn't belong and that I really didn't fit in anywhere. Today I mailed off the paperwork to open my adoption records. Although I am excited, I am also afraid. Meeting my biological parents will not take away from granny or pop-pop. I just need to meet them one time. If I can maintain a relationship with them, fine; if not, that will be fine too."

Graciously, they all responded that they would support me. That made my heart smile. I finally had something to look forward to. The glimmer of hope and expectation I had displayed in my youth was back. I was on an incredibly emotional rollercoaster, and I wasn't sure if I wanted it to end.

Chapter 7
The Longest Wait

In the meantime, my oldest son, Jeremai, had already joined a specific DNA organization. After some time with this organization, a certain gentleman had contacted him because their DNA matched very highly. After conversing a few times, my son decided to tell me about his findings. I was very excited at the thought that this man could possibly be my father! I asked my son to reach back out to this gentleman and ask him if it would be okay for me to give him a call. Needless to say, it was okay.

After speaking with this man, we both considered the possibility that, if not him, maybe one of his brothers was my father. With all that going on, I was still waiting for my original birth certificate. So, I decided to take the gentleman's advice and join the DNA organization. It took about three weeks to come back. When I finally saw the results, I knew immediately, this gentleman could not be my father. My son's numbers and mine were in the thousands; and this gentleman and I only matched in the hundreds. So, that was an indication that possibly he could be my uncle. That saddened me because all his brothers had already passed. I thought I was back at square one. There was only one positive thing I had on my side, there was still the fact that I had my birth certificate coming.

In the meantime, the gentleman was reaching out to various family members, asking them if they remembered anyone that had a baby at a very young age who might have given her up for adoption. But no one seemed to remember anything like that. The gentleman, however, was very encouraging; and he assured me, we were not going to give up until we found out who my parents were. Believe it or not this same gentleman told me he recalled a girl name Denise B. who got pregnant by one of his cousins. But he didn't know what happened to her or the baby. We didn't touch on that story too long because, in my mind, I think I had already accepted him as my uncle regardless of any outcome. I kept thinking one of his brothers had to be my father.

He had sent me a picture of a young man that actually looked exactly like my oldest son. That young man was one of his brother's sons. I found that young man on social media and informed him of my quest. Honestly, I was hoping that the young man was my brother. I always wanted a brother. That young man only knew his father's name and didn't have to much more information to offer. The gentleman sent me pictures of female relatives that I resembled. Yet no one claimed to know anything about me. Every so often, the older gentleman and I would chat and talk about possibilities for being related. He encouraged me to hang in there and not to lose the faith. I have to admit I was starting to give up. It was hard to keep the faith when every possibility came back a 'no go.'

In the trajectory of waiting for my birth certificate, the Vital Statistics returned it twice asking for more information, and a copy of a photo ID. Nonetheless, I returned it both times and waited patiently for the results. What seemed like the longest wait ever would soon come to an end. It took about five months for my birth certificate to arrive. On this day, Friday, January 4th, God heard my cries and answered my prayers! I came home to find a letter from the Vital Statistics Department sitting on my steps.

Instantly, my heart dropped. I was excited, yet afraid to open the letter because I remembered the lady saying there was a possibility my parents' names wouldn't be on the birth certificate.

I gathered all the mail and took a seemingly long and winding trip up to my bedroom. I was so nervous I almost dropped the mail a few times. I decided to take my work clothes off first and look at my other mail first. I was stalling until I couldn't stall any longer. I opened the letter and behold; all the information was there. All of it! My mother's name and age, my father's name and age were listed. My birthday, my weight at birth, and my name, "Baby Girl Brown."

I was in awe. I just couldn't contain my excitement. I needed to share what I had discovered! Immediately, I texted the gentleman I deemed my uncle, turned out, he had the same last name as my father. I asked him who David H. was? The gentleman asked, "Why are you asking?" I said, "Well, according to my birth certificate, he is my father. Immediately my phone rang; and it was the gentleman. He exclaimed, "Are you serious?" I replied ecstatically, "Yes!" He said, "David H. is my first cousin." I couldn't believe it! This was surreal. My emotions were everywhere. I couldn't believe I finally had reliable information on my biological family. I was, finally, getting answers!

Chapter 8
Where I'm From

I texted my oldest son right away. I could not believe this was happening and I needed to share the news. After 44 years, I was finally finding information about one side of my biological family. I never dreamed it would be my father's family that I would find. I always thought about my mother, not my father. All my questions have always been about her, but I welcomed all the information I could get. I was thankful for it.

The gentleman just happened to be in Paterson, New Jersey at the time we spoke, in the area where my family lives. He told me he knew where my aunt (my biological father's sister) lived and he was going to visit her the next day. That night, I could barely sleep. I was so excited; I tossed and turned all night long. The very next morning my phone rang and the gentleman, who turned out to be my second cousin, called me to let me know he was on his way to my aunt's house and that he would give me a call once he arrived. I got ready for work as I waited. I told my "newly found" second cousin I would let him know what time my break was so they could call me then. I could not wait for break. It felt like a lifetime. Low and behold, five minutes into my break my "new-found" cousin called me via FaceTime with my aunt. I was so happy I could not believe it.

My aunt was so excited she started to scream when she found out that I was alive and well. I don't know who was happier, me or her. She told me she often wondered how I was doing. She said I also had an uncle, two sisters, two great aunts, a great uncle, a niece, a great nephew and a whole bunch of cousins. Wow! I went from not having a single blood relative to gaining a whole unit in one call! The young man thought to be my brother was really my cousin. His father and my father were first cousins. I think we both were a little disappointed that we were not siblings, but we still embraced each other as cousins.

With all that happiness, I suddenly went into mourning mode. I found out my father was no longer living. My biological father passed in 1999. I also had two uncles that had passed away along with my grandparents. I found myself asking why all over again. Just when I thought I'd get to see my birth father. Why did my father have to die before I got a chance to meet him? Why did my uncles die before I met them? This time my why's were so different. This time I was sad, not angry. This is not what I'd hoped for. I always hoped, if I ever found my parents, they would still be living. My aunt told me she saw me only one time and never saw me again. She told me my grandfather (my biological mother's father) saw to it that my mother and I both got sent off, and he never told my father where we were. She also said my grandmother (her mother) was saddened by the fact she didn't have the means to take care of me.

My aunt told me my father often spoke of me with sadness in his eyes. He never got over the fact that my mother was forced to give me up for adoption without his consent. She said my one uncle often mentioned to my younger sisters that they had an older sister somewhere out here. She also told me she often wondered where I was and if I was being treated well. She wondered if I was okay. This made me very happy; it was nice to know that I wasn't forgotten. Yet, I was still trying to get over the fact that I had found my father only to lose him permanently this time. I had so many questions for my father that will never be answered. I now know he thought of me often. But, did he truly love me? Did he love my mother? Did he remember my birthday? Why did he have to go before I got a chance to meet him? What could he have told me about my mother? I feel so close and yet so far.

Unfortunately, my aunt was older than my mother, so she didn't have that much information about her. Talking to my aunt excited me, though. She told me about my uncles who passed. One was killed when he was younger, and the other one died from cancer a few years ago. She told me a little about my sisters and some of my cousins. She told me so much in one conversation. It was information overload, but I welcomed every bit of it! I was so anxious; I couldn't wait to talk to them. First, I talked to the older sister; we both were very excited. I went on social media and looked through all her pictures looking for the resemblance. It was awkward but amusing at the same time. The next day, I got to talk to my younger sister. I think she and I really look alike. That conversation was a little easier, I guess because the other sister had filled her in. It didn't seem real. I have two sisters that knew about me, even though I didn't know they existed.

I went to Barnert Memorial Hospital where I was born. Standing in front of the big brown building, I couldn't help but wish I'd been able to stay with my birth mother. I stared into the glass doors, trying to imagine her face when the doctor put me in her arms. Images of her walking out those doors with me flashed through my head. I was in my thoughts for most of the trip. Afterwards, I decided to visit my mother's last known address when she was a child. Pulling up to the front of her old house, my heart dropped. The sight of my mother's old childhood home had torn me to pieces. There were boards on the windows and graffiti everywhere. I couldn't help but wonder what happened here. On the porch steps lie a couple of junkies and alcoholics. There was trash everywhere. The front lawn was covered in beer cans, bottles, and paper bags.

I couldn't help but think, God knew exactly what He was doing when He removed me from this home. Instantly, I felt a spirit of gratitude overtake my heart. Only God knows what my life would have been like if

I was raised on the streets of Paterson by a single fourteen-year-old girl with no help or guidance. Maybe God did this to save me, but possibly, He also did it to save her.

Here I am at the hospital where I was born.

Chapter 9
Making Up for Lost Time

Talking to my aunt made me want to be a little girl again. I wanted that closeness that an aunt and niece are supposed to have. I wanted her to do my nails and my hair. I wanted to tell her all my deepest secrets. And, I wanted to make up for all the lost time, 50 years to be exact. When we talked, I did not want to hang the phone up. We have so much catching up to do. I told her how I felt, and she responded saying, "We can't change the past, we can only start today and try to catch up on some of the things that we missed." I was able to except that, after all, she was right.

My youngest son, Josh, and I decided we would take a trip to Paterson, NJ. I think he was just as excited as I was. Originally, we had planned to visit on a Tuesday, but I was so excited we visited that following Monday. There was just no time to waste! The ride was only two hours, but it seemed like an eternity. Taking that ride made me so anxious and so afraid. I didn't know what to expect. It took everything in me to keep my mind from racing with scenarios of what meeting my biological family would be like. The closer I got to my aunt's address the more nervous I felt. This was my second time returning to Paterson since I was born. The first visit was with my mother and her closest friend when I was very young, for Thanksgiving. But this place was so unfamiliar to me. It's difficult to believe, this was the place where I was born 50 years ago. In the first visit to meet my family, my son and I were only able to visit my aunt and uncle. My one sister was at work, and the other sister had taken a day trip out of town. I thought the visit would be awkward, but I felt at home around my aunt uncle. They were so welcoming. My son and I fit right in.

I just wish, I could have met my sisters that day also. Since I met my uncle, he calls me just about every day, making sure I'm okay. This really fills me up. Talking to him every day makes me feel loved. I feel like he's making sure his brother's child is well. It's a wonderful feeling, like he's my protector. Although I am very excited about everything that has come to pass, this is all so overwhelming for me. Every time I speak to my new- found family, I feel full of joy, but deep down inside I feel a little guilty. Somehow, I feel as though I am betraying the only family, I have known for 50 years. I would hope they realize that even though I found my biological family, I still love them all, and nothing will ever change that. There's a lot of mixed emotions and I just pray God will give me wisdom to deal with them.

Although I found my biological father's family, I have yet to find my biological mother or her family. I only know her name was Denise B. Unfortunately, nobody on my father side has heard from Denise since that day they last saw me, a little after birth. But I have faith that, just like I found my father's side of the family, one day I will be able to locate her as well. I was fortunate enough to speak with my second cousin who said she was my mother's best friend when they were growing up. She told me my mother was a beautiful person, and that her father was the meanest man she knew, growing up. My cousin said that when my mother got pregnant, my grandfather stopped her from going to school, until she had me. After I was born, she was able to continue school. She also told me my mother wanted to keep me, but her father told her there was no way she was bringing me in his house.

I don't know if I should be mad or grateful for him. I wonder if my grandfather ever regretted making my mother give me up. I know a 14-year-old couldn't take care of a baby without any help. If he wasn't so mean perhaps, he could have helped her. I asked my cousin where my grandmother (my birth mother's mom) was at the time. She told me my grandfather was so mean that my grandmother decided, one day, to pack her bags and leave him high and dry. It's unknown whether it was my grandmother's choice to leave my mother behind or not. I wonder if my grandfather ever stopped being mean to my mother. I wonder if or when my mother was able to get out his clutches.

My cousin told me she looked through my pictures on social media, and I look exactly like my mother. I wished my cousin and my mother would have stayed in contact with each other once they became adults. My heart breaks for her. I was so ungrateful coming up, and here it is my mother was living in hell on earth with my grandfather. I now realize, there is always somebody else in a worse situation than you. I can only imagine the pain my mother felt all alone, especially since her own mother left her there with her unbearable father. I just pray she is still alive. Then I realized something; only she, and she alone, can answer the many questions that I have in the back of my mind.

Chapter 10
A Letter to David

To my biological father:

Dear David,

Many years I have wondered where my biological family could be. Although I already had a wonderful family, I wanted to know my biological family. I wanted to know my background. Never in a million years would I have thought that I would actually find you. My heart is overjoyed with finding your family, but at the same time I am mourning your death. You never knew my name. You never knew where I was or anything about me. You never got a chance to see your baby girl or hold her in your arms.

My name is Cassandra Yvette Santiago. Mack is my maiden name. My family and closest friends call me Sand. You never knew anything about me, so I just thought I would tell you a little about myself. I finished high school and waited many years to graduate college. I have four wonderful children and six beautiful grandchildren. Yes, you are a grandfather and great grandfather. I love fried chicken wings and my favorite colors are brown and gray. I am getting to know my aunt, uncle and my two sisters. I ask them so many questions about you but it's not the same as meeting you. It can't replace knowing you for myself. Unfortunately, this is the only way I can learn about you.

My aunt told me you were a kind man that would do anything for anybody. It's heart-warming to know you were a kind spirit. My aunt also told me that you would, often, make mention of me with sadness in your eyes. It really comforts me to know that you thought about me. It's comforting to know that you cared and remembered me until your dying day. How I wish things could have turned out differently. I talk to my sisters and they tell me wonderful things about you as well. Life threw you and me an unexpected curb ball, but at the end of the day, what I do know is, my God never makes mistakes.

Father, you can rest peacefully now. I was once lost, but now I am found. And, I had a good life. I must admit, when I found out I was adopted, I didn't take it well at all. After I became an adult and began to accept things as they were, I realized that I was truly blessed. I had two wonderful parents that had done the best they could to make sure I was loved and had every tool in life that I needed to succeed. Through it all, they never gave up on me. My dad that raised me has moved on to the next life just as you have, but my mother is still here. She is alive and well and still at my side whenever I need her. I wish I could have met you, but it wasn't in the plan. I believe you were a great person just like everyone has told me. I promise you I will get to know the family and keep your name alive. I will tell your grandchildren and your great grandchildren everything I have learned about you and what I will learn.

On 4/2/19, I decided to visit your grave at the Fair Lawn Memorial Cemetery & Mausoleum. My only still-living uncle wanted the whole family to go to the grave together, but on this first trip, I had to do it by myself. I wanted to talk to you on my own. They had you for many years, and I wanted you for just a moment to myself. I had to contact the grounds keeper and find out exactly where you were, but I found you. With tears and butterflies, I stood there overlooking the place where you had been buried. I didn't realize my uncle was buried on top, so I got to visit you both. I'm standing here, asking myself how I can be so emotional when I don't even know these two guys. My heart is so heavy because two men, who are a part of me, are six feet under me. And, all I can do is talk to you through my tears. It feels like you've always been a part of my life. Kneeling at your grave, I finally got the chance to say what I have been thinking since I found your whereabouts.

Why did you have to go before I got a chance to meet you? Didn't you know that God was going to lead me to the family one day? If only you could've held on a little while longer. Can you visit me in my dreams some day? Oh, how I wish I could have met you. Uncle, you made sure everyone remembered that I existed. I am forever grateful for that. You loved me without even knowing me.

Father (David) I pray that you will join my daddy Clarence and be a part of my guardian angel circle. Not only for me, but my children and grandchildren as well. Uncle, I wish you could've met you my younger son, Josh; he looks so much like you. The resemblance is amazing. I know, if you were still alive, we would have such a close bond. You guys don't have to worry anymore. I am here, safe, and I am doing just fine. I will back soon to visit you both, and to clean off your grave. I love you both.

It's still surreal; after almost 51 years since I gave up looking, I finally found you at your final resting place. Rest on father, no more pain, no more suffering, and no more sadness. You can sleep peacefully now. Your oldest daughter, Baby Girl Brown is alive and well.

Chapter 11
Dear Mother…

Dear Mother Denise,

Where are you? Where did you go? What became of you? Are you ok? Were you able to finally get away from all the sadness and pain that your father brought on you? Did you get married? Did you have any more children? Did you connect with your own mother again? Is your father still alive? Were you able to forgive him?

I am here, alive and well. God has truly been good to me. I am so sorry to hear all the sadness that you had to endure. I am sorry that you had a father who mistreated you. I am sorry that your mother left you with your father, all alone with no one to turn to. I was told you wanted to keep me, but your father didn't allow you to. I feel like if it wasn't for my birth, you never would have gone through the extra madness that you went through. I am so sorry you had to sacrifice your happiness so I could have mine. I'm sorry you sacrificed yourself to spare my life from a world of cruelness. I want you to know, I do thank you. Only God knows what could have happened to me if you had kept me. Only God knows what you were saving me from.

Whether you were forced to put me up for adoption or not, I see it as you were just protecting your little girl. In all reality, you did what any loving mother would have done, you made sure I was safe. You made sure I was given a fair chance to have a good life. Your choice is the reason I was chosen. Don't be sad, my life wasn't too bad. I had the best of everything. And, I do understand. I understand you were just too young to raise a child on your own. I understand that you had no way to take care of me financially. I understand that you had zero support from you father. I understand you could not turn to your own mother. I understand that you just could not do it alone. I understand it all mother.

My desire for you is that you hold your head high and never regret giving me up. I was loved and nourished the way I was supposed to be. I wanted for nothing, except to know who I really was. I don't hold any judgements on you, the reason being, without you and my father, there would be no me. I wouldn't exist if God had not used the two of you. So, I say again, hold your head up high, mother; and, know that what you did was give me life. Being a mother of four, myself, helps me understand the sacrifices we have to make for our children. My father's first cousin, who was your best friend growing up, told me you loved me and that it pained you deeply to give me up. You can rest assure that I had a wonderful life, one I didn't always appreciate. My parents who raised me made sure I had everything I needed in life. They were great parents, and I couldn't have asked for better. My dad passed, but my mom is still alive and well. Presently, I may not have found you, but I know in God's time we will meet again. I have to tell you though; I found my father's family and they are wonderful. Unfortunately, I will never get to meet my father as he is in his final resting place. However, I heard so many wonderful things about him. It's easy to see why you once loved him. I know things didn't turn out the way you wanted them to turn out, but you have to know, God never make mistakes. He does everything strategically and with purpose. I am alive and well, and I pray you are too.

Chapter 12
For Adoptive Parents

Sometimes when I talk to my biological sisters, I feel excited; other times I feel like an imposter. They have each other and they had our father, but I didn't. I wasn't part of the equation, so I guess I envy them a bit because they had our father and they were all together. I know it's an adjustment for us all. I'm still trying to process it all. I am 50 and my sisters are in their thirties. I find myself wanting to do all the things that sisters do and catch up on what I missed, but distance and transportation issues makes it challenging.

I think my problem is the possibility and fear of rejection. I, recently, became a part of many adoption groups; and I see cases in which biological families reject the adopted relative. It saddens me to see that happen to others who just want to fit in and be accepted by their real families. Thankfully, this has not happened to me, all my family has embraced me with open arms, and I'm truly grateful. But, deep down, I believe I have this little fear of not being accepted myself. I know, with time I will get over this fear. I know this is something God is working out in me, so I will trust Him.

But…to the many parents that have adopted or are planning to adopt, I'd like to offer you wisdom as an adopted child. Please never withhold the critical truth from your adoptive child or children. Make sure they're age appropriate. Tell them as soon as they can understand that they are adopted. Always be as up front and honest as possible. Holding the simple truth can and will affect your child down the road. Take it from someone has been down that road. Lucky for me, with the help of God, my life was changed around for the good. But it could've been different, my ending could've been a lot worse. Had I not turned to God my life would still be a mess.

I admit, although my adoptive parents loved me, I didn't have the best support system. My parents wanted me to accept things how they were and never question any of it. That was very hard for me to do. I was just a kid, a kid with a heavy desire to know the truth. But I didn't get any type of counseling. I wasn't part of any support groups. I just had to deal with how things were thrown at me. Every child should have a right to know where they came from, if they choose to want to know.

Today in society, there are many different support groups and counselors that will assist in dealing with negative feelings from your adoptive child. The most critical thing is to talk to them. Make sure they know where they came from and the reason you adopted them. Being open and honest is better than omitting truth and causing them to resent you, their birth parents, and even themselves. Try to get as much information as physically possible about their birth parents. I know there are certain situations in which it's confidential; and certain agreements are made. But trust me when I tell you, the questions are going to come.

Listen to your child and let them know that you understand. Show them empathy. Let them lash out if they have to. If it is possible, take them to their hometown and let them see where they are from. Let them know all about their heritage. If my mother would have known some of the things that I recently found out, I think it would have made my life a little easier. Let your child know down the line, once they become an adult, they can look for their family if they choose to. This will make your life and their life a little less complicated. Don't feel that you will be replaced. You can't be, you gave them a loving and safe home that, for different reasons, their biological family couldn't.

My last advice to you is never make your child feel like they are adopted, and never let anyone in your family make your child feel like they're adopted. I mentioned earlier that my dad's grandmother would say she loved me "even if I was adopted." Parents, they don't need to hear that they are loved even if they are adopted! Please leave the "even though you were adopted" out of any sentence. Love them, unconditionally, at all times, no matter what. Let them know they were chosen! You don't have to be a blood-related parent to love a child as your own. Isn't this the reason parents should adopt? Isn't it to love their adopted children as their own? If there's any other reason outside of loving and wholeheartedly caring for a fatherless and motherless child; don't adopt. It is truly a selfless act.

Chapter 13
So, You're Adopted?

For all of you who are adopted, I have some wisdom I'd like to share with you. It's not just from what I've seen and heard, but what I've lived. So, I hope this helps, I hope you receive it because it makes no sense for you to make the same mistakes I did.

Ask as many questions as you want. Don't be afraid to share how you feel with your adoptive parents and family. If you don't feel comfortable talking to your parents, talk to a close friend or relative. Find someone with whom you can share what's on your heart. If you having trouble coping, don't be afraid to ask for counseling. There are many groups and agencies that can and will assist you in dealing with any insecurities, feelings of rejection, feelings of abandonment. Don't make the same mistakes I did. Don't hold your feelings in and act out because you don't know how to cope with your situation.

Although it's unfortunate that some adopt for malicious reasons, I believe there are more good parents that truly adopt for all the right reasons. If you are blessed enough to get great adoptive parents, cherish their love because when it's all said and done, everything happens for a reason. I know it's hard to comprehend why someone would give up their child for adoption. But, most of the time, your new environment is the better environment for you. Take it from me. Hearing how my biological mother was brought up, and how sad of a life she had, being adopted probably was the best thing that could have happened to me.

Sometimes, we don't understand when we're going through it, but we have to trust God, and I know He does not make any mistakes. Please hear me, YOU ARE NOT A MISTAKE! Even if you don't have your biological family, even if you're in a foster home, your adopted, or in the process. God created you with a very specific purpose! You matter! You deserve to be purely loved. Lastly, once you get of age you can search for your biological family. Your quest may not be the same as mine, but I know God will answer you in His time. I can only hope that your family receives you as well as my family received me. Keep the faith and leave it God's hand. I promise that it will be okay.

"When my father and my mother forsake me, then the Lord will take me up." Psalm 27:10 (KJV)

Chapter 14
My Forever Family

Mom, my forever mother; although we do not share the same DNA, you will always be my forever mother. It took me some time, but I now see that you don't have to be blood to receive and give love. No words can ever express how much I love and appreciate you. You and dad chose me, and for that I am forever grateful. For nineteen years, I gave you countless heartaches. Many times, we did not see eye to eye. Even so, you loved me when I didn't have the sense to love myself. You were always there, even when I tried to push you away. I know you couldn't understand where I was coming from because you've never had to travel this road. But I now understand, the road did not have to be as difficult as it was. I was just too young to fully grasp this.

Being chosen was a blessing. Mom, everything I am today, is because of you and dad. I know you thought I was not paying attention, but I learned so much from you. Your strength, determination, integrity, independence and unconditional love for family, is just a few traits that I am proud to say were taken from you. You are an awesome mother, grandmother, great grandmother, sister, aunt, and friend. If I could turn back in time, I would do things differently. I would embrace the fact that I was adopted. I would cherish all the moments I had with you, dad, and my sister. I would take back every mean word I uttered and every heartache I caused you.

I know you are past all that now, but I had to right all my wrongs and let you know just how grateful I am. Mom, no matter where this new journey takes me with my new found family, you don't have to fret. I am still that baby girl (the only baby girl) that was smiling the day that you and dad chose me. You're irreplaceable. You are my forever mother. I will always love you no matter who comes along.

Londie, my forever little sister, what can I say? You are, and have been, the best sister and aunt anyone could ask for. Your kind heart and your warm spirit are your best qualities. I know we have our ups and downs, but what sisters don't? You need to know I love you and I will always love you no matter what. I know I don't tell you often, but that's just me. No matter, you never have to worry about being tossed aside. For 46 years, you were my only sister, always will be. I have love in my heart for each one of you, but you will always have a special place in my heart. For you are my forever little sister.

Chapter 15
My Ongoing Journey

My journey was long, lonely and tedious, but by the grace of God, it turned out victorious for me. I still don't understand a lot, but I do understand nothing happens without God's say so. So, I am filled with expectation for everything that God has in store for me, until I just can't contain myself. It feels so good to be chosen. I, Cassandra Yvette Mack, was chosen by my parents. That's a new perspective! Having been adopted wasn't always a good feeling for me, but I can truly say to be chosen is a blessing from on High. I still don't have all the answers yet, and I may never get them; but I was chosen for a reason.

What I do know is, in due time it will be revealed. In my journey, I learned that no matter what you are going through, leave it in God's hand and He will see you through. Whatever you want, you can have, if you trust, believe, and keep the faith. Adoption doesn't have to be a setback. Just like God did it for me, He will do it for you. The

Bible says He is no respecter of persons. Even though I got partially what I prayed for, I know the other part of my prayer will be answered because He hears our prayers. I will meet my mother and her side of the family of that I am confident.

One step at a time. I started this journey with one family. Now I have been blessed with two. Although one is biological, and the other is not, nothing and nobody will ever take away the fact that they are all my family. Never give up! When it's your time God will show up.

Once upon a time, somewhere in Egg Harbor Township, New Jersey, over 44 years ago I was lost, and could not find myself. I am so grateful that, today, I am found. I was chosen. No doubt, this has been an emotional rollercoaster. I am ever so thankful to my God above for leading and guiding me through my whole ordeal. I believe I encountered every emotion that ever existed during this journey, but God's loving grace helped me endure it all. Words cannot express what I am feeling today, it's a wonderful feeling to finally have some closure on my life. I never thought this day would come as quick as it did. To be honest, even though I wanted to find my biological family, I never really asked God until about a year ago, when I wrote down my vision and made it plain.

Today I am a living witness that with God all things are possible. I went from being given away for adoption, to being specially hand-picked. Who am I? I am part Brown and part Hannibal. Who am I? I am Shirley and Clarence Mack's daughter. I am Jeremai, Jerel, Joshua, and Cierra's mother. Who am I? I am half of David H. and half of Denise B. Who am I? I am a God-fearing, strong, intelligent, exuberant, and highly favored female. I am BABY GIRL BROWN.

Made in the USA
Middletown, DE
19 May 2019